# Chapter 1: Understanding Company Culture

## Defining Company Culture

Defining company culture is essential for any organization seeking to foster an environment where employees feel engaged, valued, and motivated. Company culture encompasses the shared values, beliefs, and behaviors that shape how employees interact and work together. It is not merely about the physical workspace or company policies but rather the underlying essence of the organization that influences every aspect of operations. A strong company culture aligns with the organization's mission and vision, creating a cohesive atmosphere where employees understand their roles and feel connected to the broader objectives.

# Rise Above: The Trickle Down Effect of Company Culture

Effective company culture is built on a foundation of clear communication and mutual respect. Leadership plays a pivotal role in defining and modeling this culture. Leaders must embody the values they wish to instill, as their actions and behaviors set the tone for the entire organization. By promoting open dialogue and encouraging feedback, leaders can create a culture of transparency where employees feel comfortable voicing their opinions and contributing to decision-making processes. This inclusive approach not only enhances employee engagement but also fosters a sense of ownership among team members.

Diversity and inclusion are critical components of a thriving company culture. A diverse workforce brings a wealth of perspectives and ideas, driving innovation and improving problem-solving capabilities. Organizations that prioritize diversity and inclusion initiatives create an environment where all employees feel respected and valued, regardless of their backgrounds. This commitment to inclusivity enhances employee morale and productivity while also attracting top talent. To effectively integrate diversity into company culture, organizations must ensure that their policies, practices, and leadership reflect these values.

# Rise Above: The Trickle Down Effect of Company Culture

Measuring and assessing cultural change effectiveness is crucial for organizations that seek to adapt and thrive in a dynamic business environment. Tools such as employee surveys, focus groups, and performance metrics can provide valuable insights into how well the company culture aligns with its stated values and objectives. Regular assessment allows organizations to identify areas for improvement and implement targeted strategies that resonate with employees. As organizations evolve through mergers, acquisitions, or shifts in market dynamics, ongoing evaluation of company culture ensures that it remains relevant and supportive of employee engagement.

# Rise Above: The Trickle Down Effect of Company Culture

Finally, adapting company culture during times of transition is vital for maintaining employee engagement and morale. Mergers and acquisitions often lead to cultural clashes that can derail progress if not managed effectively. It is essential for leadership to proactively address these challenges by blending the strengths of both organizational cultures while remaining sensitive to the concerns of employees. By fostering an environment of collaboration and adaptability, organizations can navigate cultural shifts more smoothly, ensuring that employees remain engaged and committed to the new direction. Ultimately, a well-defined company culture serves as a guiding force, driving long-term success and sustainability in an ever-changing business landscape.

## The Importance of a Strong Culture

# Rise Above: The Trickle Down Effect of Company Culture

A strong organizational culture serves as the backbone of any successful enterprise, influencing not only employee engagement but also the overall performance of the organization. It encompasses the values, beliefs, and behaviors that shape how employees interact and collaborate. When a company cultivates a robust culture, it fosters an environment where employees feel valued and connected to the mission of the organization. This alignment is essential for enhancing productivity, as employees who resonate with the culture are more likely to contribute positively and remain committed to their roles.

Diversity and inclusion initiatives play a crucial role in establishing a strong culture. By embracing a wide range of perspectives and experiences, organizations can create a more innovative and adaptable workforce. A culture that prioritizes diversity not only attracts top talent but also encourages collaboration and creativity. Employees from diverse backgrounds bring unique insights, which can lead to improved problem-solving and decision-making. Therefore, fostering an inclusive culture is not merely a compliance issue; it is a strategic imperative that enhances the overall effectiveness of the organization.

# Rise Above: The Trickle Down Effect of Company Culture

Employee engagement strategies are inherently tied to the health of the organizational culture. Engaged employees are those who find meaning in their work and feel an emotional connection to their workplace. Companies that prioritize engagement understand that it is not sufficient to implement policies or programs in isolation; rather, these initiatives must be integrated within the cultural framework of the organization. Leadership plays a pivotal role in this process, as leaders who exemplify the desired culture and values set the tone for their teams. Their behavior and communication significantly influence how culture is perceived and adopted at all levels.

# Rise Above: The Trickle Down Effect of Company Culture

Mental health and well-being are critical components of a strong organizational culture. When companies prioritize the mental health of their employees, they create an environment where individuals feel safe to express their concerns and seek support. This commitment to well-being not only reduces absenteeism and turnover but also enhances overall morale. A culture that promotes mental health can drive engagement and productivity, as employees are more likely to perform at their best when they feel supported. Communication practices that encourage openness and vulnerability are essential for fostering this culture of well-being.

Finally, aligning company values with day-to-day operations is vital for sustaining a strong culture. When employees see that the actions of leadership and the organization reflect its stated values, trust is built and reinforced. This alignment is particularly crucial during periods of change, such as mergers and acquisitions, where cultural integration can determine the success of the transition. Measuring and assessing the effectiveness of cultural change initiatives allows organizations to adapt and refine their strategies, ensuring that the culture remains a driving force in achieving organizational goals. Ultimately, a strong culture not only supports employee engagement but also propels the organization toward sustained success.

## Identifying Cultural Barriers

# Rise Above: The Trickle Down Effect of Company Culture

Identifying cultural barriers within an organization is a crucial step in fostering an inclusive and engaged workplace. Cultural barriers can manifest in various forms, including implicit biases, communication styles, and entrenched practices that may not align with the organization's values. These barriers can hinder effective collaboration, employee engagement, and overall organizational performance. To effectively identify these barriers, organizations must first conduct a thorough assessment of their current culture, utilizing tools such as employee surveys, focus groups, and one-on-one interviews. This data can provide valuable insights into the perceptions and experiences of employees from diverse backgrounds, highlighting areas where cultural conflicts may arise.

# Rise Above: The Trickle Down Effect of Company Culture

One common cultural barrier is the presence of unconscious biases that influence decision-making processes. These biases can lead to the marginalization of certain groups, impacting recruitment, promotions, and day-to-day interactions. To combat this, organizations should prioritize training programs that address unconscious bias and educate employees about the impact of these biases on workplace dynamics. By fostering an environment where employees are aware of their biases, organizations can encourage more equitable practices and create a culture of inclusivity.

# Rise Above: The Trickle Down Effect of Company Culture

Communication practices also play a significant role in creating or breaking down cultural barriers. Misunderstandings often arise from differences in communication styles, whether they be verbal, non-verbal, or written. Organizations must strive to create a culture of open communication, where employees feel comfortable expressing their thoughts and concerns. Implementing regular check-ins and feedback mechanisms can facilitate better dialogue and help identify areas where communication may be falling short. Additionally, training employees in effective communication strategies can empower them to navigate cultural differences more effectively.

# Rise Above: The Trickle Down Effect of Company Culture

Leadership styles significantly impact the identification and resolution of cultural barriers. Leaders must actively demonstrate a commitment to diversity and inclusion by modeling inclusive behaviors and promoting a culture of respect. This involves not only recognizing and addressing cultural barriers but also encouraging employee participation in shaping the organization's culture. By empowering employees to voice their concerns and suggestions, leaders can gain a deeper understanding of the cultural landscape and foster a sense of ownership among team members.

Finally, measuring and assessing the effectiveness of cultural change initiatives is essential for ongoing improvement. Organizations should establish clear metrics to evaluate the impact of their diversity and inclusion efforts, employee engagement strategies, and overall cultural transformation. Regular assessments can help identify persistent barriers and inform future initiatives, ensuring that the organization remains responsive to the evolving needs of its workforce. By committing to continuous evaluation, organizations can adapt their strategies and create a thriving culture that aligns with their values and supports the well-being of all employees.

# Chapter 2: Transforming Company Culture

## Assessing Current Culture

# Rise Above: The Trickle Down Effect of Company Culture

Assessing current culture is a fundamental step for organizations aiming to foster an environment that promotes engagement, inclusivity, and overall well-being. Understanding the existing culture involves a comprehensive analysis of the values, beliefs, and behaviors that characterize the workplace. This assessment serves as a baseline, allowing leaders to identify areas of strength and opportunities for improvement. By utilizing a variety of assessment tools such as employee surveys, focus groups, and one-on-one interviews, organizations can gain valuable insights into how employees perceive their work environment and the underlying cultural dynamics that influence their engagement.

# Rise Above: The Trickle Down Effect of Company Culture

Diversity and inclusion initiatives are critical components of a healthy organizational culture. To evaluate the effectiveness of these initiatives, it is essential to assess the current state of diversity within the workforce and the inclusivity of the organizational climate. This involves analyzing demographic data, employee feedback, and retention rates among diverse groups. By understanding the experiences of underrepresented employees, organizations can identify barriers to inclusion and develop strategies that promote equitable practices. This assessment not only informs leadership of areas needing attention but also demonstrates a commitment to fostering a diverse and inclusive workplace.

# Rise Above: The Trickle Down Effect of Company Culture

Leadership styles significantly impact company culture. Assessing the current leadership approach within an organization is vital for understanding how it shapes employee engagement and satisfaction. Leaders set the tone for the work environment, influencing communication practices, decision-making processes, and overall morale. By gathering feedback on leadership effectiveness and examining the alignment between leadership behaviors and organizational values, companies can identify gaps that may hinder cultural growth. This analysis also provides a foundation for leadership development programs aimed at fostering leaders who can drive positive cultural change.

# Rise Above: The Trickle Down Effect of Company Culture

Mental health and well-being in the workplace are increasingly recognized as essential elements of a thriving organizational culture. To assess the current culture regarding mental health, organizations should evaluate the availability of resources, the openness of communication surrounding mental health issues, and employee perceptions of support. Conducting wellness assessments and promoting mental health awareness initiatives can help create a culture where employees feel safe to seek help and prioritize their well-being. This focus on mental health not only enhances employee engagement but also contributes to overall productivity and job satisfaction.

Finally, measuring and assessing the effectiveness of cultural change initiatives is crucial for ensuring that efforts lead to meaningful outcomes. Organizations must establish clear metrics and benchmarks to evaluate progress toward cultural goals. Regularly reviewing these metrics allows leaders to make data-driven decisions, adjust strategies as needed, and celebrate successes with their teams. By creating a culture of continuous assessment and adaptation, organizations can ensure that their cultural transformation efforts are aligned with their core values and responsive to the evolving needs of their employees.

## Strategies for Cultural Change

# Rise Above: The Trickle Down Effect of Company Culture

Strategies for cultural change within an organization are essential for fostering an environment where employees feel engaged, valued, and motivated to contribute to the collective success. One of the foremost strategies involves the establishment of clear and consistent communication practices. Open lines of communication enable employees to voice their thoughts and concerns, ensuring that they feel heard and respected. This transparency not only strengthens trust between leadership and staff but also aligns the organization's mission with the everyday experiences of its employees. Regular feedback loops, town hall meetings, and anonymous surveys can serve as effective tools to gauge employee sentiment and encourage a culture of continuous improvement.

# Rise Above: The Trickle Down Effect of Company Culture

Diversity and inclusion initiatives represent another critical pillar for cultural transformation. Organizations must actively seek to create a workplace that reflects a multitude of perspectives, experiences, and backgrounds. Implementing training programs that emphasize the importance of diversity and the benefits of an inclusive environment is paramount. Additionally, establishing employee resource groups can provide safe spaces for underrepresented voices, allowing for the sharing of insights and fostering a sense of belonging. By embedding diversity and inclusion into the core values of the organization, companies not only enhance employee engagement but also drive innovation through varied viewpoints.

# Rise Above: The Trickle Down Effect of Company Culture

Leadership styles play a significant role in shaping organizational culture. Leaders must exemplify the values they wish to see reflected throughout the company. Transformational leadership, which focuses on inspiring and motivating employees to exceed their own expectations, can be particularly effective in encouraging cultural change. Leaders should engage in active listening, demonstrate empathy, and provide support for mental health and well-being initiatives. By prioritizing the holistic development of employees, leaders can cultivate a culture that promotes psychological safety and encourages individuals to take risks and innovate.

# Rise Above: The Trickle Down Effect of Company Culture

Aligning company values with day-to-day operations is crucial for sustaining cultural change. This alignment requires a thorough assessment of existing practices and policies to ensure they reflect the desired culture. Organizations should integrate their core values into performance evaluations, recognition programs, and decision-making processes. This approach not only reinforces desired behaviors but also holds individuals accountable for contributing to the overall culture. Additionally, leaders should model these values consistently, reinforcing their importance through everyday actions and decisions.

Finally, measuring and assessing the effectiveness of cultural change initiatives is vital to understanding their impact. Organizations should establish key performance indicators that reflect employee engagement, turnover rates, and the success of diversity and inclusion efforts. Regular assessments can provide insights into areas requiring further attention or adjustment. By leveraging data and feedback, organizations can refine their strategies, ensuring that the cultural change not only takes root but flourishes over time. This continuous cycle of assessment and adaptation is essential for creating a resilient and thriving organizational culture.

## Engaging Employees in the Process

# Rise Above: The Trickle Down Effect of Company Culture

Engaging employees in the process of cultural change is essential for fostering an environment where they feel valued and invested. For organizations aiming to transform their culture, it is crucial to create an inclusive atmosphere that encourages participation from all levels. This begins with clear communication about the goals of the cultural shift and the role each employee plays in achieving these objectives. Transparency establishes trust, allowing employees to voice their concerns, share their ideas, and actively contribute to the change process. When employees understand the rationale behind changes and see their input taken seriously, they are more likely to embrace new initiatives and champion them among their peers.

# Rise Above: The Trickle Down Effect of Company Culture

Diversity and inclusion initiatives are a cornerstone of engaging employees, as they ensure that all voices are heard and respected. Involving employees from diverse backgrounds in the decision-making process not only enriches the cultural change strategy but also enhances employee satisfaction and retention. Organizations can create focus groups or diversity task forces that represent a wide range of perspectives, allowing employees to collaborate on solutions that best reflect the workforce's needs. This collaborative approach not only empowers employees but also fosters a sense of belonging, which is vital for their overall engagement.

# Rise Above: The Trickle Down Effect of Company Culture

Employee engagement strategies must prioritize mental health and well-being, recognizing that a healthy workforce is more productive and innovative. Organizations can implement programs that encourage work-life balance, provide mental health resources, and promote open discussions about well-being. Engaging employees in these initiatives can involve soliciting feedback on wellness programs or co-creating mental health workshops tailored to their needs. By actively involving employees in shaping these strategies, organizations can demonstrate their commitment to well-being, thereby enhancing engagement and loyalty.

## Rise Above: The Trickle Down Effect of Company Culture

Effective communication practices are fundamental to ensuring that cultural change is not only accepted but embraced. Leaders should foster an environment where open dialogue is encouraged, and feedback is welcomed. Regular check-ins, town hall meetings, and anonymous surveys can provide employees with various platforms to express their thoughts and feelings regarding the ongoing changes. Additionally, leaders should model the behaviors and attitudes they wish to see by being approachable and responsive, thus reinforcing the importance of communication in the cultural transformation process.

Finally, aligning company values with day-to-day operations is crucial for sustaining employee engagement throughout cultural change. Employees need to see a direct connection between their daily tasks and the organization's overarching mission and values. Engaging employees in this alignment process can involve workshops that explore how individual roles contribute to broader goals or recognition programs that celebrate employees living the company values. By ensuring that employees understand and actively participate in aligning their work with company values, organizations not only enhance engagement but also create a robust foundation for a thriving culture.

# Chapter 3: Diversity and Inclusion Initiatives

## The Business Case for Diversity

# Rise Above: The Trickle Down Effect of Company Culture

The business case for diversity is increasingly recognized as a fundamental pillar of organizational success, particularly in today's global marketplace. Diverse teams bring a variety of perspectives, fostering creativity and innovation that can lead to improved problem-solving and decision-making. Research consistently shows that companies with diverse workforces are more likely to outperform their peers in terms of profitability and productivity. Embracing diversity is not merely a moral imperative but a strategic advantage that can enhance an organization's effectiveness and resilience.

Inclusion initiatives play a crucial role in harnessing the benefits of diversity. Effective diversity and inclusion strategies create an environment where all employees feel valued and empowered to contribute their unique skills and experiences. This sense of belonging is vital for employee engagement, as it motivates individuals to be more committed to their work and the organization as a whole. Leadership must actively promote an inclusive culture, as their behaviors and attitudes set the tone for the entire organization. By prioritizing inclusion, leaders can cultivate a workforce that is not only diverse but also highly engaged.

# Rise Above: The Trickle Down Effect of Company Culture

Moreover, the impact of diversity on mental health and well-being in the workplace cannot be overlooked. A diverse workforce can lead to a more supportive environment, where employees feel comfortable expressing their authentic selves. This authenticity contributes to improved mental health outcomes, as employees who feel accepted and valued are less likely to experience stress and burnout. Organizations that prioritize diversity and inclusion initiatives are better equipped to support the well-being of their employees, leading to lower turnover rates and higher job satisfaction.

Communication practices are essential in driving cultural change within organizations. Leaders must ensure that the values of diversity and inclusion are effectively communicated and integrated into everyday operations. This includes transparent discussions about company goals related to diversity, providing training on unconscious biases, and creating channels for feedback. When employees understand the importance of these initiatives and see them reflected in the company's practices, they are more likely to engage with and support the cultural shift towards a more inclusive workplace.

Finally, measuring and assessing the effectiveness of cultural change initiatives is critical for sustaining progress. Organizations must establish clear metrics to evaluate the impact of their diversity and inclusion efforts. This can include employee surveys, retention rates, and performance outcomes. Regular assessment allows companies to identify areas for improvement and adapt their strategies as needed, ensuring that diversity remains a priority. By demonstrating a commitment to continuous improvement, organizations not only enhance their culture but also solidify their reputation as employers of choice in an increasingly competitive landscape.

## Developing Effective D&I Programs

# Rise Above: The Trickle Down Effect of Company Culture

Developing effective diversity and inclusion (D&I) programs is crucial for fostering an organizational culture that values and embraces differences. To initiate this process, companies must first conduct a thorough assessment of their current cultural landscape. This assessment should include gathering data on employee demographics, experiences, and perceptions regarding inclusivity within the organization. Surveys, focus groups, and one-on-one interviews can provide valuable insights into the existing barriers to inclusion. Understanding these dynamics will enable leadership to identify specific areas that require attention and to tailor D&I initiatives accordingly.

# Rise Above: The Trickle Down Effect of Company Culture

Once the assessment is complete, organizations need to establish clear objectives for their D&I programs. These objectives should align with the company's overall mission and values while also addressing the unique challenges identified in the assessment phase. Effective D&I programs are not merely about increasing representation; they should also focus on creating an environment where all employees feel empowered to contribute their ideas and perspectives. Setting measurable goals, such as improving employee engagement scores or increasing the diversity of leadership teams, will help track progress and maintain accountability.

# Rise Above: The Trickle Down Effect of Company Culture

Leadership plays a pivotal role in the success of D&I initiatives. It is essential for leaders to model inclusive behaviors and to communicate the importance of diversity in every aspect of the organization. Training programs focused on inclusive leadership can significantly impact how leaders engage with their teams and foster a culture of belonging. Leaders must also be equipped to have difficult conversations around diversity issues and to address any resistance within their teams. By demonstrating a genuine commitment to D&I, leaders can inspire others to embrace these values and contribute positively to the cultural shift.

# Rise Above: The Trickle Down Effect of Company Culture

Communication practices are critical for implementing and sustaining effective D&I programs. Organizations should prioritize transparent communication regarding D&I goals, progress, and challenges. Regular updates, town hall meetings, and dedicated channels for feedback can keep employees informed and engaged in the process. Additionally, storytelling can be a powerful tool to highlight diverse voices within the organization, showcasing the benefits of inclusivity and the experiences of employees from various backgrounds. By fostering open dialogue, organizations can cultivate a culture that values each individual's contributions and encourages ongoing participation in D&I efforts.

Lastly, the effectiveness of D&I programs must be regularly measured and assessed to ensure continuous improvement. Organizations should establish key performance indicators (KPIs) that align with their D&I objectives and regularly analyze data to gauge progress. Employee feedback, participation rates in D&I initiatives, and changes in workplace culture can serve as valuable metrics. This ongoing evaluation will help organizations adapt their strategies as needed and celebrate successes, reinforcing the importance of D&I as a core component of the company's culture. By committing to these practices, organizations can create a thriving environment where all employees feel valued, engaged, and capable of contributing to shared success.

## Measuring the Impact of D&I Efforts

# Rise Above: The Trickle Down Effect of Company Culture

Measuring the impact of diversity and inclusion (D&I) efforts is crucial for organizations aiming to foster a thriving workplace culture. Establishing clear metrics allows organizations to assess the effectiveness of their initiatives and align them with broader strategic goals. Key performance indicators (KPIs) such as employee engagement scores, retention rates, and the diversity of candidate pools can provide valuable insights into how well D&I initiatives are being integrated into the organizational fabric. By utilizing both qualitative and quantitative data, companies can gain a comprehensive understanding of the progress they are making, ensuring accountability and transparency in their efforts.

# Rise Above: The Trickle Down Effect of Company Culture

Surveys and feedback mechanisms play a pivotal role in measuring the impact of D&I initiatives. Regularly conducted employee surveys can capture perceptions of inclusivity, belonging, and overall engagement. Analyzing these responses can highlight areas needing improvement, allowing leadership to address specific concerns. Additionally, focus groups can provide deeper insights into the employee experience, enabling organizations to gather nuanced perspectives that may not be captured through standard surveys. This qualitative data enriches the understanding of how D&I initiatives resonate with employees at different levels and across diverse backgrounds.

# Rise Above: The Trickle Down Effect of Company Culture

Leadership commitment is also a critical factor in the effectiveness of D&I efforts. Organizations should evaluate how leaders are promoting and participating in D&I initiatives. Metrics such as participation rates in training sessions, attendance at diversity-related events, and the extent to which leaders model inclusive behaviors can provide insights into the cultural commitment to D&I. Moreover, aligning leadership performance evaluations with D&I outcomes encourages accountability and demonstrates that fostering an inclusive culture is a shared responsibility across the organization.

The relationship between D&I efforts and employee engagement should be closely monitored. Research consistently shows that diverse and inclusive workplaces are often more innovative and better at problem-solving. By measuring engagement levels before and after implementing D&I initiatives, organizations can assess whether these efforts translate into higher employee morale, productivity, and overall job satisfaction. Tracking these changes over time enables organizations to refine their strategies and ensure that D&I efforts are having the intended positive impact on the workforce.

Finally, it is essential to communicate the results of D&I measurements transparently within the organization. Sharing successes and challenges fosters a culture of trust and encourages ongoing dialogue about diversity and inclusion. This communication can take various forms, such as annual reports, town hall meetings, or internal newsletters. By openly discussing the impact of D&I initiatives, organizations not only celebrate achievements but also engage employees in the ongoing journey toward a more inclusive workplace. This approach reinforces the notion that D&I is not a standalone initiative but an integral part of the company culture and operational practices.

## Chapter 4: Employee Engagement Strategies

### Understanding Employee Engagement

# Rise Above: The Trickle Down Effect of Company Culture

Employee engagement is a multifaceted concept that serves as a cornerstone for thriving organizations. It encompasses the emotional commitment employees have towards their work and the organization as a whole. Engaged employees are not just productive; they are also innovative, loyal, and willing to go the extra mile to contribute to the organization's success. Understanding the nuances of employee engagement is critical for leaders and managers who seek to cultivate a workplace environment that fosters high morale, collaboration, and overall effectiveness.

At the heart of employee engagement lies a strong company culture that aligns with the values and aspirations of its workforce. When employees perceive their organization as a place where values are upheld, they are more likely to feel a deep sense of belonging and purpose. Creating an inclusive culture where diversity is celebrated not only enhances engagement but also drives creativity and problem-solving. Organizations that actively promote diversity and inclusion initiatives find that their employees are more engaged, as they feel their unique perspectives are valued and respected.

# Rise Above: The Trickle Down Effect of Company Culture

Leadership styles play a pivotal role in shaping employee engagement. Transformational leaders, who inspire their teams through vision and enthusiasm, tend to cultivate a more engaged workforce. Conversely, authoritarian leadership styles can stifle creativity and diminish employee morale. Effective leaders understand the importance of adapting their approach to meet the needs of their team members, fostering an environment where open communication and feedback are encouraged. This not only enhances engagement but also reinforces a culture of trust and collaboration.

Mental health and well-being are integral components of employee engagement. Organizations that prioritize the mental health of their employees create a supportive environment that encourages individuals to thrive both personally and professionally. This involves providing resources, such as counseling services and wellness programs, and promoting a work-life balance that allows employees to recharge. When employees feel supported in their mental well-being, they are more likely to be engaged, leading to higher productivity and reduced turnover.

Measuring and assessing employee engagement is essential for understanding its effectiveness and making informed adjustments. Various tools and strategies, including surveys and feedback mechanisms, can provide valuable insights into employee sentiment and areas for improvement. By regularly assessing engagement levels, organizations can align their practices with their stated values, ensuring that cultural change initiatives are not only implemented but also sustained over time. Ultimately, a commitment to understanding and enhancing employee engagement translates into a more resilient and thriving organization.

## Techniques to Boost Engagement

# Rise Above: The Trickle Down Effect of Company Culture

To boost engagement within organizations, several techniques can be effectively employed, each targeting specific aspects of the workplace culture and employee experience. One foundational technique is fostering open communication. Establishing a culture where employees feel comfortable sharing their thoughts and ideas can lead to greater involvement in decision-making processes. Regular town hall meetings, anonymous suggestion boxes, and open-door policies encourage dialogue, ensuring that employees feel heard and valued. This transparency not only enhances trust but also reinforces a sense of belonging, crucial for engagement.

Another vital technique is implementing diverse and inclusive practices throughout the organization. By actively promoting diversity in hiring, training, and leadership roles, companies can cultivate a workforce that reflects varied perspectives and experiences. This diversity leads to richer discussions and innovative solutions, which can enhance employee engagement. Furthermore, training programs focused on unconscious bias and cultural competency can help create a more inclusive environment where all employees feel respected and empowered to contribute.

# Rise Above: The Trickle Down Effect of Company Culture

Recognition and appreciation play a significant role in boosting engagement. Establishing a structured recognition program that acknowledges both individual and team achievements can foster a culture of appreciation. Regularly celebrating milestones, big and small, reinforces positive behaviors and motivates employees to strive for excellence. Additionally, peer recognition platforms can enable coworkers to celebrate each other's contributions, creating a supportive community that enhances overall morale.

Leadership styles significantly impact employee engagement and organizational culture. Leaders who adopt a transformational approach, characterized by inspiration, support, and active involvement in employees' growth, can create a more engaged workforce. Training leaders to develop emotional intelligence and adapt their styles to meet the needs of their teams can further enhance engagement. Cultivating a leadership culture that prioritizes mentorship and development encourages employees to invest in their roles and feel a deeper connection to the organization's mission.

Finally, measuring and assessing engagement levels through regular surveys and feedback mechanisms are essential for understanding the effectiveness of implemented strategies. Organizations should develop key performance indicators that align with their cultural goals, allowing for continuous improvement. By analyzing this data, leaders can identify areas needing attention and adapt their strategies accordingly. This ongoing assessment creates a dynamic environment where engagement is regularly evaluated, ensuring that cultural initiatives resonate with employees and contribute to a thriving organizational culture.

## Role of Recognition and Feedback

# Rise Above: The Trickle Down Effect of Company Culture

Recognition and feedback are pivotal elements in cultivating an engaged workforce and a thriving organizational culture. Employees who feel acknowledged for their contributions are more likely to be motivated and committed to their roles. This acknowledgment can take various forms, from informal praise during team meetings to formal recognition programs that highlight individual and team achievements. By fostering an environment where recognition is a regular practice, organizations can enhance employee morale and create a sense of belonging, vital components for a diverse and inclusive workplace.

# Rise Above: The Trickle Down Effect of Company Culture

The impact of feedback on employee engagement cannot be overstated. Constructive feedback serves not only as a tool for performance improvement but also as a means of reinforcing the values and behaviors that align with the organization's culture. Leaders who prioritize open communication and provide regular, meaningful feedback help to establish a culture of trust and transparency. This, in turn, encourages employees to share their thoughts and ideas, facilitating a two-way dialogue that can drive innovation and collaboration. In environments where feedback is actively sought and valued, employees are more likely to feel empowered and engaged.

# Rise Above: The Trickle Down Effect of Company Culture

Moreover, recognition and feedback are crucial in aligning company values with day-to-day operations. When leaders embody the organization's values through their recognition practices and feedback mechanisms, they set a powerful example for employees. This alignment ensures that employees understand not only what is expected of them but also how their contributions fit into the larger organizational mission. By integrating recognition and feedback into the fabric of the workplace, companies can effectively bridge the gap between stated values and actual behaviors, reinforcing a culture that reflects those values consistently.

# Rise Above: The Trickle Down Effect of Company Culture

In the context of mergers and acquisitions, the role of recognition and feedback becomes even more critical. Cultural integration is often one of the most challenging aspects of such transitions, and establishing a shared understanding of expectations and values is essential. By implementing recognition programs that celebrate contributions from both legacy organizations, leaders can foster a sense of unity and shared purpose. Additionally, providing feedback that acknowledges the strengths and opportunities of the combined workforce can help mitigate anxieties and build a cohesive culture that embraces diversity.

Ultimately, the effectiveness of recognition and feedback strategies must be measured and assessed to ensure they are achieving their intended outcomes. Organizations should regularly evaluate the impact of these initiatives on employee engagement, retention, and overall satisfaction. Surveys, focus groups, and performance metrics can provide valuable insights into the effectiveness of recognition and feedback practices. By continuously refining these strategies based on employee input and organizational goals, companies can cultivate a dynamic workplace culture that not only engages employees but also drives long-term organizational success.

# Chapter 5: Leadership Styles and Their Impact on Culture

## Overview of Leadership Styles

# Rise Above: The Trickle Down Effect of Company Culture

Leadership styles play a critical role in shaping company culture and influencing employee engagement. Understanding the various styles of leadership can help organizations align their practices with their values, fostering an environment that promotes diversity, inclusion, and mental well-being. Different leaders adopt distinct approaches based on their personalities, the dynamics of their teams, and organizational goals. This overview explores the predominant leadership styles and their implications for cultural transformation within organizations.

Authoritative leadership, often characterized by a clear vision and direction, can be highly effective in environments requiring decisive action. Leaders who adopt this style inspire their teams by articulating a compelling vision and setting high expectations. While this approach can drive performance and clarity, it may also limit employee input and creativity. Striking a balance between guiding employees and allowing them autonomy is crucial for engagement, especially in diverse workplaces where varied perspectives can enhance problem-solving and innovation.

# Rise Above: The Trickle Down Effect of Company Culture

In contrast, democratic leadership encourages participation and collaboration among team members. Leaders who embrace this style actively seek input and foster a sense of ownership within their teams. This inclusivity can lead to higher levels of employee engagement, as individuals feel valued and heard. However, democratic leadership also requires careful management of group dynamics and decision-making processes to ensure efficiency and avoid potential conflicts. Organizations prioritizing diversity and inclusion can greatly benefit from this approach, as it empowers employees from all backgrounds to contribute meaningfully to the conversation.

# Rise Above: The Trickle Down Effect of Company Culture

Transformational leadership focuses on inspiring and motivating employees by fostering personal and professional growth. Leaders in this category prioritize the development of their team members, encouraging them to exceed expectations and pursue innovative ideas. This style can significantly improve employee morale and well-being, as individuals feel supported in their career journeys. However, transformational leaders must also be attuned to the mental health needs of their employees, ensuring that the drive for high performance does not lead to burnout or stress.

Lastly, transactional leadership emphasizes structure, rules, and rewards. This style is often effective in maintaining order and achieving short-term goals but may not foster a deeply engaged culture. Organizations aiming for sustainable success must recognize the limitations of a purely transactional approach, especially in the context of cultural change. Leaders who can blend transactional elements with more inclusive and transformational practices will likely create a more adaptable and resilient workforce. By understanding and leveraging these leadership styles, organizations can navigate the complexities of cultural change and enhance overall employee engagement.

## Transformational vs. Transactional Leadership

# Rise Above: The Trickle Down Effect of Company Culture

Transformational and transactional leadership represent two distinct approaches that significantly influence company culture, employee engagement, and overall organizational effectiveness. Transactional leadership is characterized by a focus on structure, rewards, and penalties, emphasizing clear roles and expectations. Leaders employing this style prioritize task completion and performance metrics, often relying on a system of rewards for meeting objectives and consequences for failing to do so. This approach can foster a stable environment where employees understand their responsibilities, but it may also limit creativity and innovation, as the emphasis on compliance can stifle individual initiative.

# Rise Above: The Trickle Down Effect of Company Culture

Conversely, transformational leadership seeks to inspire and motivate employees by creating a shared vision and fostering an emotionally engaging environment. Leaders who adopt this style focus on building strong relationships and encouraging personal and professional growth among their team members. By prioritizing intrinsic motivation, transformational leaders can cultivate an atmosphere of trust and collaboration, where employees feel valued and empowered to contribute to the organization's goals. This approach not only enhances employee engagement but also aligns closely with diversity and inclusion initiatives, as transformational leaders are often more attuned to the unique perspectives and contributions of a diverse workforce.

# Rise Above: The Trickle Down Effect of Company Culture

The impact of leadership styles on company culture is profound. Organizations led by transformational leaders tend to exhibit a dynamic culture that adapts to change and fosters innovation, while transactional leadership can result in a more rigid culture that may resist change. In today's rapidly evolving business landscape, the ability to adapt and embrace new ideas is crucial for success. Transformational leaders are more likely to encourage open communication practices, allowing for the free exchange of ideas and feedback, which is essential for driving cultural change and aligning company values with day-to-day operations.

# Rise Above: The Trickle Down Effect of Company Culture

Furthermore, the significance of mental health and well-being in the workplace cannot be overlooked when considering these leadership styles. Transformational leaders often prioritize the well-being of their employees, recognizing that a supportive and inclusive environment contributes to overall job satisfaction and productivity. By investing in employee engagement strategies that promote mental health, organizations can create a thriving workplace culture. In contrast, transactional leadership may fall short in addressing these critical aspects, as the focus on performance metrics may overshadow the importance of employee well-being.

# Rise Above: The Trickle Down Effect of Company Culture

In the context of mergers and acquisitions, the choice between transformational and transactional leadership can greatly affect the success of cultural integration efforts. Transformational leaders are better equipped to navigate the complexities of merging distinct organizational cultures, fostering collaboration, and aligning diverse teams toward common goals. By actively engaging employees in the process and valuing their input, transformational leaders can facilitate smoother transitions and mitigate resistance. Ultimately, the effectiveness of cultural change initiatives hinges on the leadership style adopted, underscoring the importance of understanding the nuances between transformational and transactional leadership in cultivating a thriving organizational culture.

## Leading by Example

# Rise Above: The Trickle Down Effect of Company Culture

Leading by example is a fundamental principle in cultivating a robust company culture, particularly in the realms of diversity, inclusion, and employee engagement. When leaders embody the values and behaviors they wish to see in their organizations, they establish a powerful model for employees to follow. This form of leadership not only reinforces the desired culture but also fosters trust and credibility. Employees are more likely to engage with and commit to initiatives when they observe their leaders actively participating in and advocating for these efforts. Therefore, it is essential for leaders to consistently demonstrate the principles of diversity and inclusion, showing that these values are not merely aspirational but integral to the organization's identity.

# Rise Above: The Trickle Down Effect of Company Culture

In the context of mental health and well-being, leading by example takes on an even greater significance. Leaders who prioritize their own well-being and openly discuss mental health challenges can create an environment where employees feel safe to do the same. This transparency helps to dismantle stigma and encourages a culture of support, where mental health is recognized as a critical component of overall employee engagement. When leaders model healthy work-life balance, encourage regular breaks, and promote mental health resources, they signal to employees that their well-being is valued and essential for organizational success. Such actions not only enhance individual morale but also contribute to a healthier, more productive workplace culture.

# Rise Above: The Trickle Down Effect of Company Culture

Effective communication practices are also vital in leading by example. Leaders must engage in open and honest dialogue with their teams, actively listening to feedback and concerns. This two-way communication fosters a sense of belonging and encourages employees to contribute their ideas and perspectives. By sharing their own experiences and challenges, leaders can connect with employees on a personal level, reinforcing the notion that everyone is part of the same journey toward cultural change. Furthermore, when leaders communicate regularly about the organization's values and the steps being taken to uphold them, they ensure that these principles are not just words on a wall but lived experiences within the workplace.

# Rise Above: The Trickle Down Effect of Company Culture

Aligning company values with day-to-day operations is a critical aspect of leading by example. Leaders must ensure that their decisions, policies, and practices reflect the organization's stated values. This alignment creates a sense of authenticity and integrity, which is essential for building employee trust and engagement. When employees see their leaders making choices that prioritize inclusivity, equity, and employee welfare, they are more likely to feel motivated to embrace these values themselves. Moreover, this consistency helps to reinforce a culture where everyone is encouraged to contribute to the organization's mission and vision, ultimately leading to greater collective success.

Finally, during periods of change, such as mergers and acquisitions, leading by example becomes even more crucial. Leaders must navigate these transitions with transparency and sensitivity, setting the tone for how employees adapt to new cultural dynamics. By demonstrating resilience, adaptability, and a commitment to maintaining core values, leaders can guide their teams through uncertainty. This proactive approach not only helps to mitigate anxiety and resistance but also fosters a culture of collaboration and unity. In doing so, leaders affirm their role as stewards of the organizational culture, ensuring that it evolves positively and inclusively, even in challenging circumstances.

## Chapter 6: Mental Health and Well-being in the Workplace

### Importance of Mental Health in Organizations

# Rise Above: The Trickle Down Effect of Company Culture

Mental health has emerged as a critical component of organizational success, influencing not only employee well-being but also the overall culture and productivity within the workplace. Organizations that prioritize mental health create an environment where employees feel valued and supported, leading to increased engagement and retention. When mental health is treated as a fundamental aspect of company culture, it fosters a sense of belonging and empowers individuals to perform at their best. This shift not only enhances the individual employee experience but also contributes to a more cohesive and resilient organizational framework.

# Rise Above: The Trickle Down Effect of Company Culture

Incorporating mental health initiatives into the company culture is essential for promoting diversity and inclusion. Employees from various backgrounds may face unique mental health challenges, and a supportive environment acknowledges these differences. Organizations that implement comprehensive mental health strategies demonstrate a commitment to understanding and addressing the diverse needs of their workforce. This approach not only aids in attracting a wider talent pool but also cultivates an inclusive atmosphere where all employees feel empowered to share their perspectives and experiences.

Leadership plays a pivotal role in shaping an organization's approach to mental health. Leaders who model healthy behaviors and openly discuss mental health challenges set a precedent that encourages employees to prioritize their well-being. By adopting supportive leadership styles, organizations can create a culture that normalizes conversations around mental health, reducing stigma and promoting proactive measures. This cultural shift can lead to improved employee morale, higher levels of trust, and a more engaged workforce, as employees feel encouraged to seek help when needed.

# Rise Above: The Trickle Down Effect of Company Culture

Effective communication practices are vital in promoting mental health within organizations. Regular check-ins, mental health resources, and open forums for discussion can facilitate a culture where mental well-being is prioritized. Organizations should ensure that communication strategies align with their values, creating a transparent environment where employees feel safe to express their concerns. By fostering open communication, organizations can not only identify potential mental health challenges early on but also reinforce their commitment to employee well-being.

Finally, measuring and assessing the effectiveness of mental health initiatives is crucial for continuous improvement. Organizations should implement metrics that evaluate the impact of mental health programs on employee engagement, productivity, and overall company culture. Regular assessments help leaders identify areas for growth and adapt strategies as necessary, ensuring that mental health remains a priority within the organization. By committing to this ongoing evaluation, companies can demonstrate their dedication to fostering an environment where mental health is recognized as a vital component of organizational success.

## Creating a Supportive Environment

# Rise Above: The Trickle Down Effect of Company Culture

Creating a supportive environment within an organization is crucial for fostering employee engagement and promoting overall well-being. A supportive environment is characterized by open communication, respect for diversity, and recognition of individual contributions. Organizations that prioritize these elements create a culture where employees feel valued and empowered to voice their opinions and ideas. This atmosphere not only enhances employee satisfaction but also drives productivity and innovation. Leaders must actively cultivate this environment by modeling inclusive behaviors and encouraging dialogue among team members.

# Rise Above: The Trickle Down Effect of Company Culture

Diversity and inclusion initiatives play a significant role in creating a supportive workplace. Embracing diverse perspectives can lead to more creative solutions and a stronger sense of community. Organizations should implement training programs focused on unconscious bias, cultural competency, and inclusive leadership skills. Such training fosters understanding and appreciation of differences, helping to break down barriers that may hinder collaboration. By promoting a culture of inclusivity, organizations not only enhance employee engagement but also position themselves as attractive employers in a competitive job market.

# Rise Above: The Trickle Down Effect of Company Culture

Effective communication practices are essential for reinforcing a supportive environment. Leaders should establish transparent channels for feedback and discussion, allowing employees to express their thoughts and concerns without fear of repercussion. Regular check-ins, town hall meetings, and anonymous surveys can provide valuable insights into employee morale and engagement levels. Additionally, fostering a culture of recognition where achievements are celebrated can further motivate employees, creating a positive feedback loop that enhances overall organizational culture.

Aligning company values with day-to-day operations is another critical aspect of creating a supportive environment. When employees see that their organization's values are reflected in everyday practices and leadership decisions, it fosters trust and loyalty. This alignment can be achieved through regular training sessions, clear communication of expectations, and integration of values into performance evaluations. Leaders must ensure that their actions consistently reflect the company's stated values, reinforcing a culture of integrity and commitment to the organization's mission.

Finally, organizations must be proactive in assessing the effectiveness of their cultural change initiatives. Implementing metrics to evaluate employee engagement, diversity, and overall workplace satisfaction can provide valuable data for ongoing improvements. Regular assessments can help organizations identify areas for growth and adapt their strategies accordingly. By committing to continuous evaluation and adaptation, leaders demonstrate their dedication to creating a supportive environment where all employees can thrive, ultimately leading to a more engaged workforce and a thriving organization.

## Implementing Mental Health Programs

# Rise Above: The Trickle Down Effect of Company Culture

Implementing mental health programs within organizations is a critical step toward fostering an inclusive and supportive company culture. These programs are essential not only for employee well-being but also for enhancing overall productivity and engagement. Organizations must begin by conducting comprehensive assessments to identify the specific mental health needs of their workforce. This involves gathering data through surveys, focus groups, and individual interviews to understand the unique challenges faced by employees. By tailoring programs to address these needs, companies can create a more responsive and effective mental health strategy that resonates with their workforce.

# Rise Above: The Trickle Down Effect of Company Culture

Leadership plays a pivotal role in the successful implementation of mental health programs. Leaders must exemplify a commitment to mental well-being by actively participating in training and promoting open discussions about mental health. This visibility can help destigmatize mental health issues and encourage employees to seek support without fear of judgment. Training programs for leaders should include strategies for recognizing signs of distress, effective communication techniques, and how to foster a psychologically safe environment. When leadership prioritizes mental health, it sets a precedent that influences the entire organizational culture.

# Rise Above: The Trickle Down Effect of Company Culture

Communication practices are vital when implementing mental health programs. Clear and consistent messaging about the importance of mental health can help to integrate these initiatives into the fabric of the company culture. Organizations should utilize various channels—such as newsletters, workshops, and internal platforms—to disseminate information about available resources, including counseling services, mental health days, and wellness activities. It is also essential to facilitate feedback mechanisms that allow employees to voice their concerns and suggestions regarding the mental health programs. This two-way communication fosters a sense of ownership and engagement among employees, making them feel valued and heard.

# Rise Above: The Trickle Down Effect of Company Culture

Diversity and inclusion initiatives must be woven into mental health programs to ensure they meet the diverse needs of the workforce. Different cultural backgrounds may influence how individuals perceive and approach mental health, necessitating tailored interventions that respect and acknowledge these differences. Organizations should consider collaborating with mental health professionals who specialize in culturally competent care to develop programs that are accessible and relevant to all employees. By prioritizing diversity in mental health initiatives, companies can enhance participation and effectiveness, leading to a more cohesive and engaged workforce.

Finally, measuring and assessing the effectiveness of mental health programs is crucial for continuous improvement. Organizations should establish key performance indicators that align with their overall goals for employee well-being and engagement. Regular evaluations, such as employee feedback surveys and program participation rates, can provide valuable insights into what is working and what areas need adjustment. By analyzing this data, organizations can refine their mental health strategies, ensuring they remain aligned with company values and responsive to the evolving needs of their employees. Ultimately, a robust approach to mental health not only benefits individuals but strengthens the organization as a whole, leading to a thriving workplace culture.

# Chapter 7: Communication Practices for Cultural Change

## The Role of Communication in Culture

# Rise Above: The Trickle Down Effect of Company Culture

Effective communication is a cornerstone of any organizational culture, influencing not only the internal dynamics among employees but also the external perceptions of the organization. In the context of company culture, communication serves as the conduit through which values, beliefs, and practices are shared and reinforced. This sharing is essential for fostering an inclusive environment where diverse perspectives are acknowledged and valued. When communication practices are open and transparent, employees feel more engaged and empowered to contribute, which enhances overall organizational health and productivity.

Diversity and inclusion initiatives rely heavily on robust communication strategies to ensure that all voices are heard and respected. Effective communication enables leaders to articulate the importance of these initiatives, setting a tone that encourages participation and collaboration. By promoting dialogue around diversity, organizations can dismantle barriers that often inhibit open conversation. This, in turn, leads to a culture where differences are celebrated, and employees feel a sense of belonging, ultimately driving higher engagement levels and fostering innovation.

# Rise Above: The Trickle Down Effect of Company Culture

Employee engagement strategies must incorporate communication as a fundamental element to be successful. Regular feedback loops, recognition programs, and team meetings are essential practices that not only inform but also involve employees in the organizational narrative. When employees feel informed about the company's goals and their role within that framework, they are more likely to be committed and motivated. Additionally, leaders who effectively communicate their vision and expectations create an environment of trust, which is vital for sustained engagement and performance.

Leadership styles significantly impact how communication is perceived within an organization. Transformational leaders, for instance, utilize inclusive communication practices that inspire and motivate employees to embrace change. This alignment between leadership and communication fosters a culture where adaptability is prioritized, especially during times of transition such as mergers and acquisitions. Effective leaders recognize the need to communicate openly about changes, ensuring that employees understand how these shifts will affect their roles and the organization as a whole.

Finally, measuring and assessing the effectiveness of cultural change initiatives is inherently linked to communication practices. Organizations must establish metrics that evaluate not only changes in behaviors and attitudes but also the clarity and reach of their communication efforts. Surveys, focus groups, and performance metrics can provide insights into employee perceptions of culture and communication effectiveness. By continuously refining these practices, organizations can ensure that their cultural values are not only articulated but also embodied in day-to-day operations, leading to a thriving workplace that prioritizes mental health and well-being.

## Strategies for Effective Communication

# Rise Above: The Trickle Down Effect of Company Culture

Effective communication serves as the backbone of a thriving organizational culture. To foster an environment where employees feel engaged and valued, leaders must implement strategies that enhance communication across all levels of the organization. This involves not only the clarity of messages but also the inclusivity of communication practices. Organizations should prioritize transparent communication channels that encourage feedback, foster open dialogue, and create space for diverse perspectives. By establishing a culture where employees feel safe to express their thoughts and concerns, companies can enhance employee engagement and drive collective success.

# Rise Above: The Trickle Down Effect of Company Culture

Incorporating diversity and inclusion initiatives into communication strategies is essential for promoting a sense of belonging among employees. Organizations must ensure that their communication practices reflect the diversity of their workforce. This can be achieved through the use of inclusive language, varied communication methods, and tailored messaging that resonates with different demographic groups. Training initiatives focused on cultural competency can help leaders and employees alike understand the importance of inclusive communication, ultimately leading to improved relationships and collaboration within teams.

# Rise Above: The Trickle Down Effect of Company Culture

Leadership styles significantly impact communication practices within an organization. Leaders who adopt a participative or transformational approach tend to encourage open communication and empower employees to contribute to discussions. This not only enhances trust but also aligns employees with the company's values and objectives. Leaders should model effective communication behaviors, such as active listening and providing constructive feedback, as these actions cultivate a culture of respect and collaboration. By embracing a leadership style that values communication, organizations can navigate challenges more effectively and foster a more engaged workforce.

# Rise Above: The Trickle Down Effect of Company Culture

Mental health and well-being in the workplace are closely tied to effective communication practices. Organizations must prioritize mental wellness by promoting open conversations about mental health, providing resources for support, and encouraging employees to share their experiences. Regular check-ins and informal communication can help identify potential issues early on, allowing for timely interventions. By creating a workplace culture that normalizes discussions around mental health, organizations can reduce stigma and foster a supportive environment, enhancing overall employee engagement and productivity.

Finally, measuring and assessing the effectiveness of communication strategies is crucial for ongoing cultural change. Organizations should utilize surveys, feedback sessions, and performance metrics to evaluate how well communication practices align with their cultural values and objectives. This data-driven approach allows leaders to identify areas for improvement and make informed adjustments to their strategies. By continually refining communication practices based on employee feedback, organizations can ensure that they remain adaptable in the face of change, particularly during significant transitions such as mergers or acquisitions. In this way, effective communication becomes a dynamic tool for not only enhancing company culture but also driving long-term success.

## Overcoming Communication Barriers

# Rise Above: The Trickle Down Effect of Company Culture

Effective communication is the cornerstone of a thriving organizational culture. However, various barriers can hinder this vital process, impeding employee engagement and overall productivity. Addressing these barriers is essential for fostering an inclusive environment where diverse voices are heard, valued, and integrated into the company's operations. Organizations must first identify common communication obstacles, such as language differences, hierarchical structures, and cultural misunderstandings, which can lead to misinterpretations and disengagement among employees. By recognizing these challenges, leaders can implement targeted strategies to bridge communication gaps.

# Rise Above: The Trickle Down Effect of Company Culture

One significant barrier to effective communication is the presence of diverse cultural backgrounds within a workforce. While diversity can drive innovation and creativity, it can also result in differing communication styles and expectations. To overcome this, organizations should invest in cultural competency training for all employees. Such training can equip individuals with the skills necessary to navigate cross-cultural interactions, fostering an environment where everyone feels comfortable expressing themselves. Additionally, promoting an open dialogue about cultural differences can encourage employees to share their perspectives, ultimately enriching the organizational culture.

# Rise Above: The Trickle Down Effect of Company Culture

Hierarchical communication structures may also pose challenges, often creating an environment where employees feel hesitant to voice their opinions or concerns. To counteract this, leaders should adopt a more inclusive leadership style that prioritizes transparency and accessibility. By encouraging feedback and actively seeking input from all levels of the organization, leaders can dismantle the barriers imposed by hierarchy. Regular town hall meetings, suggestion boxes, and informal check-ins can serve as platforms for employees to communicate openly, helping to create a culture of trust and collaboration.

# Rise Above: The Trickle Down Effect of Company Culture

Another critical aspect of overcoming communication barriers is the alignment of company values with day-to-day operations. Organizations must clearly articulate their values and ensure that these principles are reflected in all communication practices. This alignment not only strengthens the company's identity but also reinforces a shared understanding among employees. Regularly reviewing and revising communication policies to ensure they resonate with the organization's core values can enhance cohesion and commitment among staff. Furthermore, recognizing and rewarding behaviors that exemplify these values can motivate employees to engage in more effective communication.

Lastly, organizations must measure and assess the effectiveness of their communication strategies continuously. Implementing regular surveys and feedback mechanisms can help identify ongoing barriers and areas for improvement. By analyzing this data, leaders can make informed adjustments to their communication practices, ensuring they remain relevant and effective in a dynamic workplace. As employees see their feedback being valued and integrated into organizational practices, their engagement levels are likely to increase, contributing to a healthier, more productive company culture. In overcoming communication barriers, organizations can create an environment where every employee feels empowered to contribute, ultimately driving success and growth.

# Chapter 8: Aligning Company Values with Day-to-Day Operations

## Defining Core Values

# Rise Above: The Trickle Down Effect of Company Culture

Defining core values is a fundamental step in shaping an organization's culture and guiding its strategic direction. Core values represent the deeply held beliefs that drive an organization's behavior, influencing decision-making processes and employee engagement. By articulating clear core values, organizations can establish a unified identity that aligns with their mission and vision, fostering a sense of belonging among employees. This alignment not only enhances employee morale but also serves as a compass for navigating the complexities of workplace dynamics, particularly during times of change such as mergers and acquisitions.

# Rise Above: The Trickle Down Effect of Company Culture

In the context of diversity and inclusion initiatives, core values play a critical role in promoting an inclusive workplace culture. Values centered around respect, equity, and collaboration encourage diverse perspectives and foster an environment where all employees feel valued and heard. Organizations can leverage their core values to create policies and practices that support diversity, ensuring that every employee has equal opportunities for growth and development. By embedding these values into the organizational fabric, companies can enhance employee engagement and retention, ultimately leading to higher levels of innovation and productivity.

# Rise Above: The Trickle Down Effect of Company Culture

Leadership styles significantly impact how core values are perceived and enacted within an organization. Leaders who exemplify and advocate for core values set the tone for the entire workforce, influencing employee behavior and cultural norms. Authentic leadership, characterized by transparency and integrity, is particularly effective in reinforcing core values. When leaders consistently model these values, they inspire trust and commitment among employees, enhancing overall engagement. Furthermore, effective communication practices are essential for ensuring that core values resonate with employees at all levels, making them integral to everyday operations.

# Rise Above: The Trickle Down Effect of Company Culture

Aligning company values with day-to-day operations is crucial for sustaining cultural change. When core values are consistently reflected in organizational practices, policies, and employee interactions, they become a living part of the corporate culture. This alignment not only motivates employees but also fosters a strong sense of accountability, as individuals understand that their actions directly contribute to the organization's mission. Regularly assessing and measuring the effectiveness of cultural change initiatives can help organizations identify areas for improvement and reinforce the importance of core values in achieving long-term success.

In conclusion, defining core values is a foundational element that underpins an organization's culture and operational effectiveness. By establishing clear, meaningful values and integrating them into all aspects of the workplace, organizations can cultivate an environment that promotes employee engagement and well-being. As companies navigate the challenges of modern business, a strong commitment to core values will not only enhance their internal culture but also position them as leaders in their respective industries.

## Integrating Values into Operations

Integrating values into operations is a critical strategy for organizations seeking to foster a culture of engagement, inclusivity, and high performance. When employees perceive that their organization's values are genuinely reflected in everyday practices, they are more likely to feel a sense of belonging and commitment. This alignment between stated values and operational practices is essential for cultivating an environment where employees feel empowered to contribute meaningfully. Leaders play a pivotal role in this integration process by modeling behaviors that exemplify the organization's core values, thereby setting a standard for others to follow.

# Rise Above: The Trickle Down Effect of Company Culture

To successfully embed values into operations, organizations must first ensure that these values are clearly articulated and understood by all employees. This involves not only defining the values but also communicating them consistently throughout the organization. Training programs, workshops, and internal communications should reinforce these values, making them an integral part of the organizational narrative. By engaging employees in discussions about how these values manifest in daily work, organizations can foster a deeper understanding and commitment to them. This clarity is particularly crucial in environments undergoing change, such as during mergers or acquisitions, where a unified understanding of values can bridge cultural differences.

# Rise Above: The Trickle Down Effect of Company Culture

Moreover, it is imperative for organizations to develop systems and processes that support value-driven decision-making. This can include incorporating values into performance metrics, evaluation criteria, and reward systems. For instance, recognizing and rewarding employees who exemplify core values in their work not only reinforces the importance of these values but also motivates others to align their behavior accordingly. Furthermore, engaging employees in the development of these systems can enhance their ownership and commitment to the values, resulting in a more cohesive and engaged workforce.

# Rise Above: The Trickle Down Effect of Company Culture

Effective communication practices play a significant role in the successful integration of values into operations. Leaders must be transparent in discussing how values influence strategic decisions and operational practices. Regular feedback loops, open forums, and surveys can facilitate a culture of dialogue where employees feel safe to express their thoughts and experiences regarding value alignment. By actively seeking input and addressing concerns, organizations can demonstrate their commitment to not only espousing values but also living them. This two-way communication fosters trust and strengthens the connection between employees and organizational leadership.

Finally, assessing the effectiveness of value integration requires a systematic approach. Organizations should implement tools and metrics to measure how well values are being integrated into everyday operations and the overall impact on employee engagement and organizational culture. This ongoing assessment enables organizations to identify areas for improvement and adapt strategies as needed. By continually evaluating and refining their approach to integrating values, organizations can ensure that they remain relevant and responsive to the needs of their employees, ultimately leading to a thriving organizational culture that supports engagement and productivity.

## Assessing Alignment and Consistency

# Rise Above: The Trickle Down Effect of Company Culture

Assessing alignment and consistency within an organization is crucial to fostering an environment where engaged employees can thrive. It begins with a clear understanding of the company's core values and how these values translate into everyday practices. Organizations must evaluate whether their policies, procedures, and behaviors are in harmony with the stated values. This alignment not only strengthens the company culture but also enhances employee trust and commitment. Regular assessments, including employee surveys and feedback mechanisms, can provide valuable insights into how well the organization embodies its values in practice.

# Rise Above: The Trickle Down Effect of Company Culture

Diversity and inclusion initiatives serve as a critical focal point for assessing alignment and consistency. Organizations that prioritize these initiatives must ensure that their hiring practices, training programs, and workplace policies reflect a commitment to diversity. Conducting audits of these programs can help identify gaps between intentions and outcomes. For instance, examining representation at various levels within the organization can reveal areas where alignment may be lacking. By taking actionable steps to address these discrepancies, organizations can create a more inclusive culture that resonates with their diverse workforce.

# Rise Above: The Trickle Down Effect of Company Culture

Leadership styles play a pivotal role in shaping company culture and must be assessed for their effectiveness in promoting alignment. Leaders are often seen as the embodiment of organizational values, and their behavior sets the tone for the workplace environment. By evaluating leadership approaches, companies can determine if they are fostering a culture that encourages engagement and collaboration. Training programs that focus on adaptive leadership styles can enhance leaders' ability to connect with employees, thus reinforcing the alignment between values and daily operations. This evaluation helps in identifying leaders who exemplify the desired culture and those who may require further development.

# Rise Above: The Trickle Down Effect of Company Culture

Mental health and well-being in the workplace are integral to assessing cultural alignment. Organizations must evaluate whether their practices promote psychological safety and support for employees. This includes examining the availability of mental health resources, work-life balance policies, and stress management programs. By soliciting employee feedback on these aspects, organizations can determine if their support systems are effective and align with the cultural values they aim to promote. A strong commitment to mental health not only enhances employee well-being but also contributes to a more engaged and productive workforce.

Finally, measuring and assessing cultural change effectiveness is essential for ensuring sustained alignment and consistency. Organizations should implement key performance indicators (KPIs) that reflect both qualitative and quantitative measures of cultural health. Regular reviews of these metrics can help identify trends and areas for improvement, allowing companies to adapt their strategies accordingly. In the context of mergers and acquisitions, it is particularly vital to assess how well the merging cultures align and what changes may be necessary to create a cohesive environment. By prioritizing ongoing assessment, organizations can navigate cultural transformations more effectively and ensure that engagement remains at the forefront of their strategic objectives.

## Chapter 9: Adapting Company Culture During Mergers and Acquisitions

### Challenges of Merging Cultures

# Rise Above: The Trickle Down Effect of Company Culture

Merging cultures within organizations presents a complex array of challenges that can significantly impact employee engagement and overall organizational effectiveness. When two companies with distinct cultures come together, the potential for conflict arises as differing values, beliefs, and practices interact. Employees may feel a sense of loss or uncertainty, leading to decreased morale and productivity. This disruption can be particularly pronounced when the merger is perceived as a threat to individual or collective identities, making it essential for leadership to recognize and address these feelings proactively.

# Rise Above: The Trickle Down Effect of Company Culture

One of the primary challenges in merging cultures is the potential clash between leadership styles. Different organizations often have varying approaches to management, decision-making, and employee relations. These disparities can lead to confusion and frustration among employees, who may struggle to adapt to a new leadership paradigm. Effective leaders must navigate these differences by fostering open communication and promoting a shared vision that aligns with the merged organization's goals. By doing so, they can help create a cohesive environment that encourages collaboration and mitigates resistance to change.

# Rise Above: The Trickle Down Effect of Company Culture

Another significant hurdle is the integration of diversity and inclusion initiatives. Each organization may have its own strategies and policies in place, which can complicate the merger process. Employees from diverse backgrounds may feel marginalized if their unique perspectives are not adequately represented in the new culture. It is crucial for leadership to prioritize inclusivity and ensure that all voices are heard during the cultural integration process. By implementing comprehensive training programs and establishing employee resource groups, organizations can create an environment that values diversity and fosters a sense of belonging.

# Rise Above: The Trickle Down Effect of Company Culture

Communication practices play a vital role in addressing the challenges of merging cultures. Transparent and consistent communication helps build trust among employees and alleviates anxiety associated with uncertainty. Leaders must actively share information about the merger, its implications for employees, and the steps being taken to integrate cultures. Regular feedback loops should be established to gauge employee sentiment and adjust strategies accordingly. By fostering a culture of open dialogue, organizations can facilitate smoother transitions and encourage employee engagement throughout the merger process.

Finally, measuring and assessing the effectiveness of cultural change initiatives is essential for understanding the impact of the merger on employee engagement and organizational health. Leaders should establish clear metrics that reflect the success of cultural integration efforts, such as employee satisfaction surveys and retention rates. Continuous evaluation allows organizations to identify areas for improvement and make necessary adjustments. By actively engaging employees in this assessment process, organizations can empower them to contribute to the evolving culture, ultimately leading to a more resilient and thriving workplace.

## Strategies for Successful Integration

# Rise Above: The Trickle Down Effect of Company Culture

Successful integration of new strategies into an organization requires a multifaceted approach that considers the unique aspects of company culture, employee engagement, and leadership dynamics. The first step in this process is to conduct a thorough assessment of the existing culture, identifying both strengths and areas for improvement. This assessment should involve employees at all levels, ensuring diverse perspectives are included. Engaging employees in surveys or focus groups can provide valuable insights into how initiatives are perceived and what changes might resonate most effectively within the organization. This participatory approach not only fosters a sense of ownership among employees but also lays the groundwork for a more inclusive environment.

# Rise Above: The Trickle Down Effect of Company Culture

Once the assessment is complete, it is essential to align the integration strategies with the organization's core values. This alignment ensures that any new initiatives are not viewed as isolated changes but rather as extensions of the company's mission and vision. Leaders play a crucial role in this process by clearly communicating how these strategies support the overarching goals of the organization. Consistent messaging from leadership reinforces the significance of cultural change and demonstrates a commitment to embedding these values into daily operations. Moreover, when employees see that initiatives are genuinely tied to the company's ethos, they are more likely to engage with and support them.

# Rise Above: The Trickle Down Effect of Company Culture

Effective communication practices are paramount in facilitating successful integration. Organizations should develop a comprehensive communication plan that outlines how changes will be communicated throughout the organization. This plan should include multiple channels to reach diverse employee groups, ensuring that messages are accessible and resonate with various demographics. Regular updates, feedback loops, and open forums for discussion can further enhance transparency and trust. By fostering an environment where employees feel comfortable expressing their thoughts and concerns, organizations can address potential resistance and adapt strategies as needed.

# Rise Above: The Trickle Down Effect of Company Culture

In addition to communication, training and development initiatives should be a cornerstone of the integration strategy. Providing employees with the necessary tools and resources to navigate changes is vital for fostering engagement and adaptability. This may include leadership training that emphasizes inclusive leadership styles, workshops focused on diversity and inclusion, and mental health awareness programs. Empowering employees through education not only enhances their skills but also reinforces the organization's commitment to employee well-being and a supportive workplace culture.

# Rise Above: The Trickle Down Effect of Company Culture

Finally, it is essential to establish metrics to measure the effectiveness of cultural change initiatives. Organizations should develop key performance indicators that align with their specific goals and objectives, allowing for ongoing assessment and adjustment of strategies. Regularly evaluating progress against these metrics not only helps in identifying successes but also highlights areas for improvement. By adopting a continuous feedback mechanism, organizations can remain agile and responsive to the evolving needs of their workforce, ensuring that integration efforts lead to sustainable cultural transformation.

## Maintaining Employee Engagement

# Rise Above: The Trickle Down Effect of Company Culture

Maintaining employee engagement is a critical component of fostering a thriving organizational culture. It requires a multifaceted approach that aligns with the company's values and promotes inclusivity, well-being, and effective communication. Organizations must cultivate an environment where employees feel valued, heard, and connected to the company's mission. This sense of belonging can be achieved through regular feedback loops, recognition programs, and opportunities for professional development that empower employees to grow and contribute meaningfully to the organization.

# Rise Above: The Trickle Down Effect of Company Culture

Diversity and inclusion initiatives play a vital role in enhancing employee engagement. When employees see themselves represented and feel that their unique perspectives are valued, they are more likely to invest in their work and the organization's goals. Companies should actively seek to create diverse teams and promote an inclusive culture that celebrates differences. This involves training leaders to recognize unconscious biases, implementing policies that support equitable opportunities, and fostering open dialogue among employees to ensure that everyone feels comfortable sharing their ideas and concerns.

# Rise Above: The Trickle Down Effect of Company Culture

Leadership styles significantly influence employee engagement and overall company culture. Transformational leaders, who inspire and motivate their teams, can cultivate a sense of ownership and commitment among employees. By engaging in active listening and providing transparent communication, leaders can build trust and encourage collaboration. It is essential for leaders to model the behaviors they wish to see in their teams, demonstrating empathy and resilience, particularly during times of change or uncertainty. This approach not only enhances engagement but also contributes to a positive workplace atmosphere.

# Rise Above: The Trickle Down Effect of Company Culture

Mental health and well-being in the workplace are increasingly recognized as pivotal in maintaining employee engagement. Organizations must prioritize the mental health of their employees by providing resources such as counseling services, wellness programs, and flexible work arrangements. Encouraging a culture of openness around mental health can help to destigmatize these conversations and promote a supportive environment. Leaders should actively check in with their teams, fostering a culture where employees feel comfortable discussing their well-being without fear of judgment or repercussions.

Lastly, measuring and assessing the effectiveness of cultural change initiatives is essential to maintaining employee engagement. Organizations should implement regular surveys and feedback mechanisms to gauge employee sentiment and identify areas for improvement. By analyzing this data, leaders can make informed decisions that align with the needs and expectations of their workforce. Continuous assessment allows organizations to adapt and refine their engagement strategies, ensuring they remain relevant and effective in a dynamic work environment. This commitment to ongoing improvement not only strengthens engagement but also reinforces the organization's dedication to its core values and mission.

# Chapter 10: Measuring and Assessing Cultural Change Effectiveness

## Key Performance Indicators for Culture

# Rise Above: The Trickle Down Effect of Company Culture

Key Performance Indicators (KPIs) for culture serve as essential tools for organizations aiming to evaluate and enhance their workplace environment. These metrics provide quantifiable data that can be analyzed to gauge the effectiveness of cultural initiatives, employee engagement strategies, and diversity and inclusion efforts. By establishing clear KPIs, organizations can better align their day-to-day operations with their core values, leading to a more cohesive and purpose-driven workplace. Tracking these indicators allows leadership to identify areas for improvement, celebrate successes, and ensure that cultural change initiatives are making a meaningful impact.

# Rise Above: The Trickle Down Effect of Company Culture

One of the primary KPIs for measuring company culture is employee engagement scores. Surveys that assess employee satisfaction, commitment, and emotional investment in their work can provide valuable insights into the overall culture of an organization. High engagement scores typically indicate a positive workplace culture, where employees feel valued and motivated. Conversely, low engagement scores can signal underlying issues that may require immediate attention, such as poor communication practices or a lack of alignment between company values and employee experiences. Regularly monitoring engagement scores also enables organizations to observe trends over time, making it easier to identify the effects of implemented cultural changes.

# Rise Above: The Trickle Down Effect of Company Culture

Diversity and inclusion initiatives are another critical aspect of company culture that can be quantitatively assessed through specific KPIs. Metrics such as the diversity of hiring pools, retention rates of underrepresented groups, and participation in training programs on unconscious bias can highlight how effectively an organization fosters an inclusive environment. By setting targets for these indicators, leadership can hold themselves accountable for progress and ensure that diversity and inclusion remain top priorities. Additionally, tracking these metrics not only enhances organizational culture but also demonstrates a commitment to social responsibility, which can improve the company's reputation and attract top talent.

# Rise Above: The Trickle Down Effect of Company Culture

Leadership styles significantly influence company culture, and KPIs can help measure their impact on employee morale and organizational effectiveness. Metrics such as employee turnover rates, team performance assessments, and feedback on leadership effectiveness can provide insights into how different leadership approaches affect cultural dynamics. For example, a leadership style that encourages open communication and employee participation may lead to higher levels of trust and collaboration among team members. Conversely, a more authoritarian approach may stifle innovation and engagement, ultimately detracting from the desired culture. By assessing these KPIs, organizations can refine their leadership development programs to cultivate styles that align with their cultural goals.

Finally, assessing mental health and well-being within the workplace is increasingly recognized as a vital KPI for measuring organizational culture. Metrics such as absenteeism rates due to mental health issues, employee wellness program participation, and employee feedback on work-life balance can provide a comprehensive view of how well an organization supports its employees' well-being. A culture that prioritizes mental health not only enhances employee satisfaction and productivity but also contributes to a more resilient workforce. By incorporating these KPIs into their evaluation processes, organizations can create a culture that emphasizes well-being, ultimately leading to improved overall performance and employee retention.

## Tools and Techniques for Assessment

# Rise Above: The Trickle Down Effect of Company Culture

Tools and techniques for assessment are vital for organizations aiming to foster an engaged workforce and cultivate a thriving culture. Understanding the current state of company culture is essential for driving meaningful change. Various assessment tools can be employed to gauge employee sentiment, organizational values, and the effectiveness of diversity and inclusion initiatives. Surveys, focus groups, and interviews are among the most commonly used methods. Each tool offers unique insights into employee experiences and perceptions, allowing leaders to identify areas for improvement and tailor strategies accordingly.

# Rise Above: The Trickle Down Effect of Company Culture

Surveys are a powerful tool for collecting quantitative data on employee engagement and cultural alignment. By utilizing well-structured questionnaires, organizations can measure factors such as job satisfaction, perceived inclusivity, and alignment with company values. Regularly administering these surveys enables organizations to track progress over time and benchmark against industry standards. The key to effective surveys lies in crafting clear, relevant questions that encourage honest and thoughtful responses, thereby ensuring the data collected is both actionable and reflective of the workforce's true sentiment.

# Rise Above: The Trickle Down Effect of Company Culture

Focus groups provide a qualitative approach to assessment, allowing for deeper exploration of employee experiences and perspectives. In a group setting, employees can share their thoughts on company culture, leadership styles, and the effectiveness of engagement strategies. This format encourages rich dialogue and can uncover insights that surveys may miss. Facilitators play a crucial role in guiding discussions and creating a safe environment for open communication. By synthesizing the findings from focus groups, organizations can develop a nuanced understanding of cultural dynamics and identify specific areas that require attention.

# Rise Above: The Trickle Down Effect of Company Culture

Interviews, while more time-consuming, can yield invaluable insights into the individual experiences of employees. One-on-one conversations allow for a deeper exploration of personal narratives related to diversity and inclusion, mental health, and well-being. Leaders can use interviews to uncover the stories behind the data, gaining a comprehensive view of how policies and practices impact employee engagement and satisfaction. This personalized approach not only enhances understanding but also fosters trust and demonstrates a genuine commitment to addressing employee concerns.

To effectively measure and assess cultural change, it is essential to integrate these tools into a continuous feedback loop. Organizations should not only implement assessments but also act on the insights gained. Establishing metrics for cultural change effectiveness, such as tracking participation rates in initiatives or monitoring employee turnover, can help organizations evaluate the impact of their efforts. By aligning assessments with strategic goals and regularly revisiting the findings, leaders can ensure that their initiatives contribute to a positive and enduring cultural transformation, ultimately leading to a more engaged and thriving organization.

## Continuous Improvement in Cultural Change

# Rise Above: The Trickle Down Effect of Company Culture

Continuous improvement in cultural change is essential for fostering an environment where employees feel engaged, valued, and motivated to contribute to the organization's success. This process begins with an unwavering commitment from leadership to embrace and advocate for a culture of inclusion and diversity. Leaders must model the behaviors they wish to see, demonstrating transparency, accountability, and respect for differing perspectives. By creating an organizational ethos that prioritizes continuous improvement, leaders lay the groundwork for a cultural transformation that resonates throughout the entire company.

# Rise Above: The Trickle Down Effect of Company Culture

To effectively implement continuous improvement, organizations must establish clear communication practices that promote transparency and encourage feedback. Open dialogue allows employees to voice their concerns and suggestions, fostering a sense of belonging and ownership in the cultural change process. Regular surveys, focus groups, and town hall meetings can serve as platforms for gathering insights and assessing the pulse of the organization. By actively listening to employees and responding to their feedback, organizations can refine their initiatives and ensure they remain aligned with the evolving needs of their workforce.

Moreover, aligning company values with day-to-day operations is crucial for sustaining cultural change. This involves integrating core values into every aspect of the organization, from hiring practices to performance evaluations. When employees see a direct correlation between the company's stated values and their everyday experiences, they are more likely to engage with and support those values. Continuous improvement in this area requires ongoing training and development opportunities that empower employees to embody these values in their work, thereby reinforcing a cohesive organizational culture.

# Rise Above: The Trickle Down Effect of Company Culture

The role of mental health and well-being in the workplace cannot be overlooked in discussions of cultural change. Organizations committed to continuous improvement must prioritize the mental health of their employees by creating resources and support systems that promote well-being. This includes offering mental health days, access to counseling services, and fostering a work environment that encourages work-life balance. By showing genuine care for employees' mental health, organizations not only enhance engagement but also cultivate a culture of empathy and support that can significantly improve overall morale and productivity.

# Rise Above: The Trickle Down Effect of Company Culture

Finally, measuring and assessing the effectiveness of cultural change initiatives is vital for ensuring continuous improvement. Organizations should develop metrics that evaluate employee engagement, retention rates, and the overall impact of diversity and inclusion initiatives. By analyzing these metrics regularly, leaders can identify areas for improvement and celebrate successes, fostering a culture of achievement. Continuous improvement in cultural change is not a one-time endeavor but an ongoing journey that requires commitment, adaptability, and a willingness to learn from both successes and setbacks.

www.ingramcontent.com/pod-product-compliance
Lightning Source LLC
Chambersburg PA
CBHW062107220526
45471CB00010B/3638